EVERYBODY DON KOLOMENTAL

Tolu' A. Akinyemi

First published in Great Britain as a
softback original in 2021

Copyright © Tolu' A. Akinyemi
The moral right of the author has been asserted.
All rights reserved.

No part of this publication may be reproduced, stored in a retrieval system, or transmitted, in any form or by any means, without the prior permission in writing of the author, nor be otherwise circulated in any form of binding or cover other than that in which it is published and without a similar condition including this condition being imposed on the subsequent purchaser.

Editing and Proofreading
Hungry Bookstore

Cover Design: Buzzdesignz

Published by 'The Roaring Lion Newcastle'
ISBN: 978-1-913636-11-1

Email:
tolu@toluakinyemi.com
author@tolutoludo.com

Website:
www.toluakinyemi.com
www.tolutoludo.com

ALSO, BY Tolu' A. Akinyemi from
'The Roaring Lion Newcastle'

"Dead Lions Don't Roar" (A collection of Poetic Wisdom for the Discerning Series 1)

"Unravel your Hidden Gems" (A collection of Inspirational and Motivational Essays)

"Dead Dogs Don't Bark" (A collection of Poetic Wisdom for the Discerning Series 2)

"Dead Cats Don't Meow" (A collection of Poetic Wisdom for the Discerning Series 3)

"Never Play Games with the Devil" (A collection of Poems)

"A Booktiful Love" (A collection of Poems)

"Inferno of Silence" (A collection of Short Stories)

"Black ≠ Inferior" (A collection of Poems)

"Never Marry A Writer" (A collection of Poems)

DEDICATION

To everyone dealing with mental health and life's struggles. You're not alone.

Contents

Acknowledgements 1

Poems 2

   My Voice Is Too Loud 3

   Men Don't Cry.. 4

   My Ex Is Looking for Me 5

   Mental 6

   Suffering and Smiling... 7

   Mood Swings 8

   Competition 9

   A Single Story 10

   Bachelorhood... 11

   No Pity 12

   Bitter Kola 13

   Self-Doubt 14

   Stung 15

   Strange Bedfellows.. 16

   Checkmate 17

   Best Friend... 18

   Burning 19

Conversations with the Dead 20
Gone with the Wind 21
Kingmaker 22
Don't Snap It Yet 23
People of the World 24
Bitterness 25
Voices 26
Therapist in Need of Therapy 27
Gossip 28
Public Service Announcement 29
Sad and Lonely 30
Binned 31
Burnt 32
My Girls 33
Hope Is Not Far Away 34
Guilty as Charged 35
Therapy 36
Clock of Life 37
Success 38
Hope Is Not Dead 39
Everybody Don Kolomental 40
Be a Strong Man 41
The Tenth Chapter 42

Bio	43
Author's Note	45
Dead Lions Don't Roar	46
Dead Cats Don't Meow	48
Unravel Your Hidden Gems	50
Dead Dogs Don't Bark	52
Never Play Games With The Devil	54
A Booktiful Love	56
Inferno of Silence	58
BLACK ≠INFERIOR	60
NEVER MARRY A WRITER	62

Acknowledgements

Sincere appreciation to God Almighty for the wisdom to write yet another poetry collection.

I attest to the supremacy of the Almighty God, the giver of wisdom. Without him, I'm nothing.

To my darling wife, Olabisi – Thanks for accepting my taunts about my iconic status gracefully and always being a shoulder of support whenever I churn out these gems. For always giving me a listening ear, I'm very grateful.

Sincere appreciation to my son (the math professor) – Isaac, for the genuine smile on your face when you saw Daddy putting finishing touches on yet another book. You will get used to the title – someday.

To my beautiful daughter, Abigail – I love you more than I can express in words. You're my special girl.

To my parents, Gabriel and Temidayo Akinyemi – Thanks for everything. To my fellow literati, Olushola and Oluseyi, don't stop writing.

A final thanks to everyone who has supported me on this journey that keeps unravelling so many booktiful experiences.

POEMS

My Voice Is Too Loud

My silence is an earthquake. Erupts noisily
in a bubble of fury.

The doctor says I am introverted. Sounds like a walking
time-bomb. Beautiful and melancholic. *The medications*, he
says, *release your bottled-up emotions every fortnight.*

Felt like a shit of uncontrollable faeces, threatening to soil
my white jeans.

This is driving me to the edge – a cliff-hanger. Like a bomb
about to explode in my own face.

My boss gave me a sack letter, says, *You're too famous to
be my handyman.* I echoed, *I will do anything to put food
on the table.*

Anything?

Clean up my mess then, she says.

Men Don't Cry

I cried a river beneath high walls and the tears discoloured the walls.

The tears were silent tears. Unseen like the invisible particles that killed the macho man in the high-rise on 44th Avenue.

Thirty years ago, Mother said, *Boys don't cry.* I inhaled my tears like dust.
        Deeply.

Freddie, my neighbour, died in a pool of tears.
Every day, I cry a bucket of emotions whenever my strings are drawing blanks.

My Ex Is Looking for Me

I heard my ex is looking for me.

Says *I'm an incomplete project. Owe her two kids.*

I smash things. Break tables with iron legs.
Uncomplimentary words send me out of control
like burning fire in brimming heat.

The memories flood in like ocean waves.
How she broke me, left with a man who left her
like abandoned goods from a failed robbery scene.

My ex is looking for me, but I'm nowhere to be found.

Mental

How do I tell father I have hit a stone wall?
Without a label like a tightly fastened seatbelt
on a driver of a speeding car.

How do I tell mother my mental health is failing like a car without brakes?
Without her heart pumping blood like a revving car
at turbo speed.

How do I tell this religious leader that I am in a dark place?
Without some imaginary demons getting more than five vicious blows.

How do I find healing in tranquillity?
Without being judged through a blurry lens.

Suffering and Smiling

We are shuffling, suffering and smiling.

Our shuffling feet's straying is the hallmark of intense hustle.

Some shuffled for survival till they met their Waterloo.

Our suffering could be found in open places. Ninety-nine standing in molue buses like tightly packed sardines.

Upgraded us to Lagos BRTs, one step higher than the devil and the deep blue sea.

Still, we smiled. The statistics won't kill us. Won't steal our joy. Won't take our shine.

They rubbed salt in our wounds. Inflicted more pain. Still, we radiated joy, smiling even in intense pain.

Suffering and smiling is our bittersweet tale.

Mood Swings

My mood is swinging like a flickering fluorescent bulb.
There are days I'm on a high like a visionary
ready to hold the world by its collar.

You can call me a mysterious child on some nights
when I feel like mashed potatoes.

Many times, I feel overwhelmed and overweight
with the burden of the universe so heavy
hanging on my beleaguered shoulders.

My mood draws apposite. Goes to war in divergent
directions. Calls me the greatest.
Livens my dead spirit

                      until my mood swings the other way.

Competition

Nicole the daughter of Nzeribe sent two cars from Italy last week. *You're here like matter, adding weight and occupying space.* Those words hit harder than tremor.

How do I tell Papa that Nicole's twigs are dried out?
Her shrubs are no longer green.

Amaka has two children. Her home is as noisy as carnival grounds. Words escaped out of the tightly shut window.

How do I tell Papa that Amaka was laid to rest last week?
The neighbours say she was scrubbed off the earth
by her dearest husband.

A Single Story

Swallows deep like a manhole.

A singular story sells false narratives like a monopoly with no competitor.

The man who died in the city centre last night was a victim of jungle justice.

This morning, they broke the news with trembling lips. The cries of *thief, thief, thief* that rended the air were a hoax.

The mob set him ablaze before he could patch up the fallacies.

He was a victim of a single story.

Bachelorhood

My bachelorhood looks like a time-stamp that can't be erased. The single sisters are ducking.

My romantic lines are missing their targets.
Two inches to the left. Falling flat.
Short.

They say my wallet is not as deep as the Atlantic Ocean.

Who cares about a bright future?

My bachelorhood has no expiry date.

These spinsters on the run are
forebodings of great danger.

No Pity

I have lost all sense of feeling for men of little means.
Hounded me for bread.
Two loaves. Five loaves.

Still not enough.
Hounded me for survival.

Had sex with Maria; she gave birth to twin boys. Hounded me for upkeep as if I gave the green light the night he parted her legs like the Red Sea.

I have lost all sense of honour for perennial beggars. Lost my goodwill after they left me for years. For dead.
                                                          Forgotten.

Hollered out of the blues. Hello, Cheerful giver.
I play deaf and dumb.
                          Then mute, deaf and dumb.

Before I unleash the block button.

Bitter Kola

I threw out all my friends from middle school. They tasted like grandpa's bitter kola in brown calabash.

Bitter.

The spittle was as thick as a fur. With a wry smile.
The same smile grandpa wore when he crunched
the bitter kola and blood stained his tongue.

He scurried into the inner room like a child in need of attention. His teeth left a bitter mark.

Gritting my teeth like grandpa.

I threw out one last spittle, to ensure there were no remnants.

Self-Doubt

One doubt.

Bury me with my unbelief.

Ripe like fresh bananas.

Kill me in the ocean of doubt.

One atom of doubt is enough to send me on a downward spiral.

Never allow me to wallow in this cloud of pity that seeks to extinguish my rising star.

Two doubts.

Don't drown me in a Moana of fear before my last dance.

Self-doubt killed the great warrior in Sidon before his enemies arrived with a wooden bow – and no arrows.

Stung

My billionaire uncle was a stingy cat.
But we were poor like church rats.
He says all the poor do is lament and cry.

Dump their garbage on the rich.
Hit a brick-wall and you're classed a villain.

Then lament over again.

My billionaire uncle preached *patience is a golden tool*.
Now I borrow from his book of wisdom when I'm labelled
a stingy cat for billions I never had.

I say words like *Time is Life, Use it Wisely*. But my words
escape into thin air and I'm stung by the label,

>   which hurts like stinging darts.

Strange Bedfellows

Her love language was like that of the choir mistress –
pitch high soprano lifting weary souls.

Only on Sundays, in church, screaming in a fit of ecstasy.
She's found her lover – Jesus. Everyone is happy.
I go home languid, sulking; my right hand has no nails.

Eating away slowly – trying to unravel her love language.

Checkmate

My mental health is on the brink. I passed out for twenty seconds at the sight of the ocean beneath Third Mainland Bridge. The urge to jump in overwhelmed my being. Like a stronghold. Failed swimmer.

Life-long dreamer.

Failing at this life fling. The great beyond isn't a choice, though life has been raining thorns.

The rain of abuse is over-flooding my being. These dark strings are pulling at my soul. Sorrowful love affair.
                              Not soulful.

The wrinkles are a sign.
Dark lines not from youthful exertions.
Just dark lines.

Best Friend

My best friend no longer wishes me well. Sees my success as normal. Evades my success stories like a plague.

Rotting away in a pit of failure.

My best friend's tongue is a pile of filth. Buried me alive and fed me to the dogs in a blink.

Ate my carcass for dinner in one chunk.

My best friend has no name. Wiped away without footprints by the bitterness in their heart.

Burning

The dark pit in my head is a burning furnace.
These demons are having a field day.

Roasted like plastic on wasteland. These voices are a menace.
Pummelled by invisible forces, body sticky like clay.

Conversations with the Dead

I carry a portrait of my grandmother in my mind.

Her memory evergreen.

Broke the news in bits, *your favourite gran died.*

Unbelievable, forever gone.

I converse with the dead on my off days.

Her portrait lightens me up like sun rays.

Gone with the Wind

The rustling wind in summertime stood still.

His bubbling face is no longer here.

Run of the mill, dearest old Bill.

His vivid footprints, wiped – no longer there.

Gone with the wind.

One of a kind.

Kingmaker

The kingmaker in Lagos fathered many children out of wedlock. They are now royals. Warlords.

Conquering territories.

His wife says, *He is not a cheat.*
Not a dead-beat.
Never say dead meat.
Anyone who births greatness is a hero.

She says, *Give him the red carpet and one royal crown.*

They say, *She is out of her mind.*
Lost the plot and the thick of the story.

Don't Snap It Yet

This swirling. These hallucinations.
These haunting shadows are like a thick cloud.

The unending worries are an ocean bed. The weight of fear thuds like the volcano that left Pacaya in ruins.

Your body is a country with no borders. You say you have lost the war. Say tomorrow might be your last.

    Rock bottom.

Don't snap it yet.
    The little flicker might light this city.
  Breathe. Breathe out the debris that clogs the wheel of your happiness.

People of the World

Are waiting to chew on your grief like hungry lions and spit
    out the carcass when the stomach no longer rumbles.

Are waiting to hear your sad tales splashed on lips
    screaming, *We don't wish you well*.

Are waiting to see you fall from high altitudes like a plane
    crashing into the Mediterranean Sea. Send in half-
    hearted commiserations.

Are waiting to laugh at your grace-to-grass story. Pretend
    they care before they do what people of the world do.

Bitterness

Twenty great kings were drowned in the ocean of bitterness.

And five fiery goddesses were consumed by their envious hearts.

The leaves turned yellow and fell off in spring. That was a bad sign.

Mama named her *Purity,* but the only thing pure was the white dress she wore on her wedding day.

Her heart had a bitter stain from the venom in her filthy tongue.

Voices

The voices in my head pump up my adrenaline. I take two blows to the head. Land on the canvas.
Back glued to the ground.

Stifling.

I heard a chorus of boos. The voices flood in like a torrent of rain. Say, *This is where you belong*.

The canvas.

The voices in my head sing a song of hope. Duck the right jab. Take five body-blows and land an upper right.

Champion.

Therapist in Need of Therapy

My therapist is in need of therapy. Switch off your mic.

This truth is raining fury.

My therapist is an addict. Gambles and loses. Sell things. Auctioned his ancestral home for ten shillings. Sold the small fridge. His wedding gift. That was the straw that ended his dream wedding. His wife left in the dark. Says she is scared; she might be up for sale in the general market.

My therapist is unstable. Like Manchester's weather. Someday he will rain truth

                            before he spirals out of control.

Gossip

His mouth needs super glue to seal it up for good. It's
    raining cats and dogs of other people's secrets.

Eats the wood of Auntie Shanty's hut like a termite. That
    night, the smiles that pour from his face are a rhapsody
    of delight.

My head is leaking stories that sends my adversaries into
    overdrive. They say, *He's blown.* Started as a rookie.
    Made jest of him in our group chats. Called him
    names.

Jester.

Thought he was a chancer. Soon fade. Now we are dried
    like plantain chips from the words we've sown.

Public Service Announcement

My favourite uncle is running a riot in the land of the dead. Left before sunset. Truly never lived. The memories are a haunting blur.

Harvard trained.

Burnt lips from smokes. Chronic addict. Blue chinos caught fire from ciggies. Called the fire service, survived – never burnt alive.

They whispered he was demon possessed. Some days he was free like a bird. Others, he was trapped in a dingy hole.

Broken man like cracked eggs. Held captive in the throes. They say he was losing his mind.

The stigma was never erased.
Inadequate. Incapable. Inconsequential.

Sad and Lonely

My darling girl is sad and lonely. Started a pity-party, no guests and Nigerian Jollof. Sent her away, still with no pity.

Gave her two currencies of self-belief to bank. Spend. She left with a smirk.

And a smiling face.

Binned

My bank balance cried in French and Swahili.
Foreign tongues left me dazed.
Felt like strange lightning.

Binned a few no-do-gooders.
They were like a pit.
Needy for faeces.

Sucked me like fresh orange juice.
I dug a hole.
And binned them for life.

Burnt

My head is a burning wood. The ashes are smoking hot.
   Darkened clouds – smells like vengeance.

The gods are angry. Don't call them family. The ingrates
   who chopped off my father's left finger. Sucked the
   blood. Laughed it off and screamed blue murder.

My head is a cracking frame. Like a broken puzzle. The
   hero in their cracking game.

My Girls

My girls are trading blows.
Brought hammers to a fistfight.
The casualties are countless.

Hate residue lies on our doormat.
Sang *Hallelujah, Hosanna in the highest*.
Hypocrisy stinks like rotten apples.

My girls are fighting dirty.
This mud fight has cost one arm and two ounces of joy.

They will spit fire before we are all burnt by fireworks.

Hope Is Not Far Away

Who will tell Okikiola that tomorrow is pregnant?
        Like a mother hen with unhatched eggs.

Who will tell Okikiola that hope is not far away?
        Its ship docked in the home of Akinyele
before his candle was blown out and his flailing dreams
were a shipwreck.

Who will tell Okikiola this is not the last straw?
        These wind gusts would give way for the
calming sea.

Who will tell Okikiola that this is not the last bus stop?
        Hope is not far away, and this is not the end.

Guilty as Charged

They said my favourite artiste was a rapist. Sentenced in the court of public opinion.

No lawyers. No defence. No jury.

Cancelled. Guilty as charged.

Who makes a case against the raging fury of this clandestine movement?

A rape allegation is sacrosanct.
You're either guilty or guilty.

Izu has gone to the land of no return. He was sent away, no resistance, no clap-backs.

Just a raging inferno that started from a matchstick.

Nailed to the cross.

The end.

Therapy

My mind is blowing hot and cold.
Like a standing fan in a hot room.
In this city, they say therapy is for the weak.

Weakness has no name. No colour. Respects no one. The addict who walked the length of this city naked was the son of the governor.

Died in an orgy. Who says therapy is a curse? For the weak, timid men without limbs.

Purge your minds at the revival ground.
    After cleansing with oil.
The demons would scurry like a rat back into hiding.

My head is blowing hot and cold.
Till I'm washed clean by oil, no bottles.

Just therapy.

Clock of Life

The clock has run its full course.
Look at the honours.
Like five Olympic medals in the trophy cabinet.

The clock's chime respects no one. It yells like ferocious thunder at the north end of the Palace of Westminster.

They say, *Big Ben is always in a fit of rage.*
Yelling. Shouting. In fury.

Amuses revellers. With fancy cameras, striking colourful poses.

The clock of life chimed non-stop when the devil's first son breathed his last after eating the forbidden apple.

Success

Success visited the home of that small boy from fifth grade.

No flex.
    Swag or camaraderie.

Ate me deep. Had me for breakfast.
Convulsed through the day and hit my head on the wall all evening.

Next morning, my heart felt heavy.
Like a drowning body.
    Floating…

Hope Is Not Dead

We drank from the nozzle of hope when life's deep gulley threatened to swallow us like a vicious whale.

Hope is not dead: Our trembling lips kept its flame alive.

They said there was no hope. A dead end like an unending tunnel.

Hope is not dead: Our quaking tongues bellowed in unison.

The one who dealt hope a crushing blow spent the rest of his life on a lowly low.

Everybody Don Kolomental

Voices pitch-high like clanging metals.
Coloured faces scattered with uncooked dreams.
We roamed bubbling streets under the burning heat. We roamed fully clothed. We roamed and roamed in search of succour.

Everybody Don kolomental.

Our suffering faces were scattered with glitters of hope.
      Tomorrow go better – we hung our dreams on the frames of tomorrow.

Everybody Don kolomental.

Everybody gets craze. Some minute, others overflowing like a running stream. Depression is an abominable word. Hush it, they chorused.

Never give the devil a chance.
Depression is another word for a roaming devil that invades your heart with pitch darkness.

Everybody Don kolomental.

Our madness was hidden beneath colourful clothes. A little scuffle is all it takes to unravel the different layers.

Be a Strong Man

Say hard as a stone.
When her words were like a hot knife on butter.

Piercing through the core of his soul.
He was built to last, tailor-made to withstand the fiery storm.

When the vicissitudes of life rained hail and thunderstorms.
Bruised
        and battered.
They say, *Be as strong as a rock.*
A strongman is like a strong tower.

He was a strongman until he withered away.

The Tenth Chapter

My fictional work is discussed in hush tones. Labelled with a stamp – highly classified secrets.

What a farce!

Work of fiction. Artistic imprint. Call me nightcrawler. When men slept, worked overtime.

Built dreams from the rubbles of imagination.

My shadow looms larger than your favourite poet. They say he is not deep.

Not our next rated. I'm an African giant. Hang my frame next to Bukowski.
Greatness doesn't bask in vain validation.

Control.Alt.Delete.

Don't erase my evergreen footsteps, so vivid in the sands of time as we close this tenth chapter.

Bio

Tolu' A. Akinyemi (also known as Tolutoludo & Lion of Newcastle) is an award-winning Nigerian author in the genre of poetry, short story, and essays, which include: *Dead Lions Don't Roar* (Poetry, 2017), *Unravel Your Hidden Gems* (Essays, 2018), *Dead Dogs Don't Bark* (Poetry, 2018), *Dead Cats Don't Meow* (Poetry, 2019), *Never Play Games With The Devil* (Poetry, 2019), *Inferno of Silence* (Short Stories, 2020), *A Booktiful Love* (Poetry, 2020), *Black ≠ Inferior* (Poetry, 2021), *Never Marry a Writer* (poetry, 2021), and *Everybody Don Kolomental* (Poetry, 2021).

Tolu' has been endorsed by the Arts Council England as a writer with "exceptional talent". A former headline act at Great Northern Slam, Crossing The Tyne Festival, and Feltonbury Arts and Music Festival, he also inspires large audiences through spoken word performances. He has appeared as a keynote speaker in major forums and events and facilitates creative writing master classes to many audiences.

His poems have appeared in the 57th issue (Volume 15, no 1) of the *Wilderness House Literary Review*, *The Writers Cafe Magazine* Issue 18, GN Books, Lion and Lilac, and elsewhere.

His books are based on a deep reality and often reflect relationships and life and features people he has met in his journey as a writer. His books have inspired many people to improve their performance and/or their circumstances. Tolu' has taken his poetry to the stage, performing his written word at many events. Through his writing and these performances, he supports business leaders, other aspiring authors, and people of all ages interested in reading and writing. Sales of the books have allowed Tolu' to donate to charity, allowing him to make a difference where he feels its important, and to show that he lives by the words he puts to page.

He is a co-founder of Lion and Lilac, a UK-based arts organisation.

Tolu' is a financial crime consultant as well as a Certified Anti-Money Laundering Specialist (CAMS) with extensive experience working with leading investment banks and consultancy firms.

He is a trained economist from Ekiti State University, formerly known as University of Ado-Ekiti (UNAD). He sat for his master's degree in Accounting and Financial Management at the University of Hertfordshire, Hatfield, United Kingdom. Tolu' was a student ambassador at the University of Hertfordshire, Hatfield, representing the university in major forums and engaging with young people during various assignments.

Tolu' Akinyemi was born in Ado-Ekiti, Nigeria and lives in the United Kingdom. Tolu' is an ardent supporter of Chelsea Football Club in London.

You can connect with Tolu' on his various social media accounts:

Instagram: @ToluToludo
Facebook: facebook.com/toluaakinyemi
   Twitter: @ToluAkinyemi

Author's Note

Thank you for the time you have taken to read this book. I hope you enjoyed the poems in it.

If you loved the book and have a minute to spare, I would appreciate a short review on the page or site where you bought it. I greatly appreciate your help in promoting my work. Reviews from readers like you make a huge difference in helping new readers choose the book.

Thank you!
Tolu' Akinyemi

Dead Lions Don't Roar

In a society where moral rectitude is increasingly becoming abeyant, Akinyemi's bounden duty is to reawaken it with verses. He, thus, functions as a philosopher-poet, a kind of factotum inculcating wisdom in different facets of life. Dead Lions Don't Roar leads us into the universe of an exact mind rousing the lethargic from indolence or prevarication, bearing in mind that the greatest achievers are those who take the bull by the horn. Taking a step can just be the open sesame to reach the stars. Enough of jeremiad! - **The Sun**

Dead Lions Don't Roar, a collection of poetic wisdom for the discerning, makes an interesting read. A paper pack, the poems are concise, easy to digest, travel friendly and express deep feelings and noble thoughts in beautiful and simple language. -**The Nation**

Akinyemi's verses are concise, straight-edge and explanatory, reminiscent of the kind of poetry often churned out by Mamman J. Vatsa, the late soldier and poet. –**yNaija**

Dead Lion's Don't Roar is a collection of inspiring and motivating modern-day verses. Addressing many issues close to home and also many taboo subjects, the poetry is reflective of today's struggles, and lights the way to a positive future. The uplifting book will appeal to all age groups and anyone going through change, building or enjoying a career, and facing day to day struggles. Many of the short verses will resonate with readers, leaving a sense of peace and wellbeing.

Dead Cats Don't Meow

In all, this poetry collection *Dead Cats Don't Meow* generally emphasizes the theme of self-belief and taking action. It reminds me of the saying "if you think you are too little to make an impact, try staying in a room with a mosquito." - **BellaNaija.**

Overall, *Dead Cats Don't Meow* comes across as a collection of thoughtful poetry that inspires, entertains, and educates its reader. It is a great blend of themes spanning across love, inspiration, politics, entrepreneurship, marriage and life, among others. Its simplicity eludes intentionality, and the plays on words show experience.

The collection is suitable for both the literary and non-literary community and is a great work for all manner of readers. I believe, with this one, Akinyemi has achieved his goals of motivation.

- The Nation Newspaper.

Dead Cats Don't Meow urges its readers not to waste their ninth life…the author of the collection of poetic wisdom for the discerning adds his third compendium of poems to the bookshelves alongside *Dead Lions Don't Roar* and *Dead Dogs Don't Bark*. Tolu A. Akinyemi, renowned poet, author and performer, brings to us *Dead Cats Don't Meow*, a metrical masterpiece which invokes love and respect for life with every word. Each poem examines a part of life, a sensation, a reaction, or an emotion. Beautifully written…individually, the verses breathe their own beat, whilst the collection knits together perfectly to present an idyllic collection to attain innate potential. "Don't waste the ninth life! Don't miss the chance to add this rare compendium of poetic wisdom to your bookshelf today!"

Unravel Your Hidden Gems

Unravel Your Hidden Gems is like a Solomon talking to us in the 21st century. The book teaches us to value what we have, the pursuit of excellence, and, above all, steps to unravel your hidden gems, drawn from your extraordinary talents, deposited in you right from the first day the placenta was severed from the womb. A book for all seasons, no doubt, especially in Africa where aspirations sometimes do not match inspirations, it is only logical that you add it to your shopping cart. **- Guardian Arts**

Watching others ascend the totem pole of life with relative ease, some come to believe they can't fly. Times without number, they have tried, yet they have found no way to break the ice. Don't despair if you are unsettled by a losing streak.

Tolu Akinyemi, the author of *Unravel Your Hidden Gems,* believes that the hero lies in you. If only you can discover the hidden gems in you, you are on your way to excelling. How, then, do you dig deep into the labyrinth for the gems?

Unravel Your Hidden Gems is a 376-page book by a prolific UK-based Nigerian author. It is a collection of over 360 inspirational and motivational essays from a young man who feels he has a mission to rouse dampened spirits to make the much-needed push in life to regenerate abundantly.

In seven parts, the author makes a diligent search into typical problems encountered by men, capable of weighing them down, and comes up with snippets of wisdom. **- The Sun**

Unravel your Hidden Gems is a collection of inspirational and motivational essays from the heart of the acclaimed author, Tolu' A. Akinyemi. Released hot on the heels of Tolu's first book of poetry, *Dead Lions Don't Roar*, this new book is a study on Life, encouraging people to succeed at what they feel is important to their own happiness. Be it private life, business, religion, career, or relationships, each part of life is discovered. This mind-altering life manual can be read as a whole or visited in snippets for day to day inspiration. Each essay examines and highlights challenges in life and how to succeed in enjoying life with grace. A self-help study on life with a refreshing difference, the book is a totality of life's journey, reminding us we are here on a temporary basis and that it is our duty to not hide in obscurity, but to Unravel Your Hidden Gems before it is too late! Pure Inspiration!

Dead Dogs Don't Bark

Dead Dogs Don't Bark is as culturally relevant as can be, and this deserves commendation. – **Bellanaija**

In a nutshell, Dead Dogs Don't Bark is enjoyable, it is stimulating. - **Bdaily UK**

The collection takes this reader through an exhilarating journey of wits and pun. The power of words, both grand and subtle, is that it allows the reader to place himself in the scheme and feel the poems on a more visceral level. Creating concrete imageries, the poet says even before it sticks out its tongue and bares its teeth, the first thing that defeats a fainthearted in an unfamiliar threshold is the bark of a dog. It sends cold shivers running down the spine. That very bark, disarming as it is, is the dog's way of calling attention: I am here! **- Guardian Arts**

Dead Dogs Don't Bark is the second poetry collection from the acclaimed author Tolu' A. Akinyemi. With a similar tone and style *to Dead Lions Don't Roar* (Tolu's first poetry collection) this follow-up masterpiece is nothing short of pure motivation. The poems cover a range of topics that many in life are aware of, that the Author himself has experienced and that we all, whatever our age, need support in.

Beautifully written, the poems speak volumes to all age groups as they feature finding your inner talent and celebrating your individuality and distinct voice. The poetry collection has didactic elements for evaporating the effects of peer pressure and criminality amongst many others. Also covering mental health, relationships, career focus, and general life issues, the poetry is bittersweet, amusing, and thought-provoking, in turns.

Never Play Games With The Devil

TOLU' A. AKINYEMI

Reflective, insightful, and ultimately inspirational, *Never Play Games with the Devil* is a collection best digested slowly and thoughtfully. It's a series of insights and admonitions about life's purposes and coping mechanisms for *"...not crashing under the weight of the world."*
D. Donovan, Senior Reviewer, Midwest Book Review

Readers will find Akinyemi's reflections on significant life issues completely relevant, sharply logical, and deeply felt. -

The Prairies Book Review

Hear the poet as, in a succinct moment of self-adulation, he writes:

"My brain thinks faster than my words can convey. My mind works magic. Can I live this life forever?"

Divided into three sections, *Never Play Games with the Devil* showcases a poet at the height of his powers, exploring several themes in different voices.

In the first section, the poet is the charismatic preacher encouraging people to Hustle, Find their Feet and Grow. He writes about the lot of Broken Men crashing under the weight of expectations; he talks about boys like Eddie and Edmund, bullied for the shape of their heads. He humorously addresses the consequence of choices in the title poem, 'Never Play Games with the Devil.'

The second section secures him a seat as an activist. We see the poet tackle, in verse, despotic and undemocratic governments, marauding killer herdsmen, and the pastor who lost his voice. The poet mourns the hapless souls in the crossfire between society's rot and the State's insouciance.

The final poems explore the basis of human relationships. The poems here deal with love, commitment, and trust.

Never Play Games with the Devil is a didactic collection of poems on pertinent life issues. These poems draw their appeal from the poet's ability to sustain a figment of thought through the entire span of each poem.

A Booktiful Love

Poet Tolu' A. Akinyemi tackles life with a passionate, analytical, observing eye and creates admonitions which pull at emotional strings in the heart. Poetry readers who choose his free verse collection will find it equally powerful whether it's considering divorce and grief or the love language of 'A Booktiful Love'. - **D. Donovan - Senior Reviewer, Midwest Book Review.**

Readers will find Akinyemi's collection an intriguing approach to exploration of the entirety of human experience in its various forms. This is a superb collection. - **The Prairies Book Review.**

A Booktiful Love is a collection of poems that deal with the entirety of human experience in its various forms. Didactically rich, the poems explore ideas ranging from love, relationships, and patriotism to marriage, morality, and many other concepts pertinent to daily living.

Given its variety of themes, what unifies the poems in this collection is the simplicity and ambiguousness of language which the poet employs. The poems draw their strength from their clarity and meaning.

These are poems with a purpose. Poet Tolu' A. Akinyemi didn't shy away from this fact, as he wrote in the poems "Writers" and "Write for Rights." The poet's philosophy is evident in this collection. To him, a writer is saddled with the responsibility to use his words to teach, preach, and fight for freedom.

He writes:

"Let's change the world, one writer at a time,
Write those words till the world gets it right."

Another special attribute to this collection is the poet's experimentation with words. This is clear right from the title. The poet identifies himself as a creator of words. The reader is obliged to travel into the mind of the writer in each poem, to understand how his mind works. As readers approach the end of this collection, they not only become engrossed in its didactic richness, but also will appreciate the uniqueness of the poet's style and the sense of responsibility he carries.

Inferno of Silence

Inferno of Silence is a wide-ranging collection that tackles different themes of love, life, interpersonal relationships, and social and political challenges. It's a hard-hitting, revealing collection that keeps readers engaged and thinking with each short exploration of characters who confront their prejudices, realities, and the winds of change in their lives.

Readers of literary explorations that include African cultural influence and modern-day dilemmas will find this collection engrossing. - **D. Donovan, Senior Reviewer, Midwest**

Book Review

Poignant and honest...

Akinyemi's first collection of short stories dazzles with elegant prose, genuine emotions, and Nigerian cultural lore as it plumbs both the socio-cultural issues and the depths of love, loss, grief, and personal trauma. Lovers of literary fiction will be rewarded. - **The Prairies Book Review**

The first collection of short stories by this multitalented author entwines everyday events that are articulated in excellent storytelling.

The title story "Inferno of Silence" portrays men's societal challenges and the unspoken truths and burdens that men bear, while "Black lives Matter" shows the firsthand trauma of a man facing racism as a footballer plying his trade in Europe.

Stories range from "Return Journey" where we encounter a techpreneur/ Poet/Serial Womanizer confronting consequences of his past actions, to "Blinded by Silence," where a couple united by love must face a political upheaval changing their fortune.

These are completed with stories of relationships: "Trouble in Umudike" – about family wealth and marriage; "Everybody don Kolomental" where the main character deals with mental health issues; and "In the Trap of Seers" when one's life is on auto-reverse with the death of her confidante, her mother, as she takes us through her ordeal and journey to redemption. This is a broad and very inclusive collection.

BLACK ≠INFERIOR

Akinyemi employs a steady hand and heart to capturing Black lives in various nuances, from political and social arenas to personal experience: *"Equality is a forgotten child. The blood of the innocents/soil the World. Racial Injustice walks tall,/the graves of our ancestors quake in anguish/at this perpetual ignominy."*

This juxtaposition of the personal and the political makes *Black#Inferior* a particularly important read. It holds a compelling, accessible message to the Black community in the form of hard-hitting poems which offer emotional observations of the modern state of Black minds and societies around the world.

Poetry readers interested in the fusion of literary ability and social inspection will appreciate the hard-hitting blend of both in *Black#Inferior,* which is recommended reading for a wide audience, especially students of Black experience.- *D. Donovan - Senior Reviewer, Midwest Book Review.*

A celebration of black culture and experience and life in general, the collection makes for an electrifying read. - *The Prairies Book Review.*

Black ≠ Inferior is a collection of poems divided into 2 parts. The first part is a collection of thematically linked poems exploring Blackness and the myriads of issues it attracts. The second part oscillates themes— talking about consent, a query of death, a celebration of love among others. In his usual stylistic, this collection deals with weighty matters like race and colourism with simple and clear language.

In Black ≠ Inferior, we see Tolu' Akinyemi reacting in response to the world, to issues that affect Black people. Here, we see a poet shedding off his burdens through his poems; hence, the beauty of this collection is in the issues it attempts to address. In this collection, Tolu' wears a coat of many colours – he is a preacher, a prophet, a doctor and a teacher.

We see Tolu' the preacher in these lines:
'I wish you can rise through the squalor of poverty and voices that watercolour you as under-represented. I wish you can emblaze your name in gold, and swim against every wave of hate.'

This is a collection of poems fit for the present narrative as any (Black) person who reads this collection should beam with confidence at the end. This is what the poet sets out to achieve with his oeuvre.

NEVER MARRY A WRITER

Ultimately, the poet's caution to "Never Marry a Writer" is a deeper disclaimer, a warning that is more a promise. Writers, these poems remind the reader, bear witness. Whether evocative prose or colorful whimsy or the bleakest of forthright documentation, their words attest to the truths they observe. With its wily wordy ways, this collection reminds readers that even those without a literary spouse are nevertheless subject to--and on notice from--those who, like the author, observe and document. --- "The US Review of Books" (RECOMMENDED by the US Review)

"Bold, wry, and lyrical musings." -- *Kirkus Reviews*

OH, THE WEBS WE WEAVE...

For his seventh poetry collection, Tolu' has turned his attention to that old adage -
no one in a writer's life may have secrets.
A vibrant, human exploration of the way in which words and deeds connect all of us, and the tiniest movements which span out across continents.

Tolu' writes powerfully on family, love, loss, and with a scorching curiosity for the world around us. His readers will be familiar with his inimitable style, and this latest collection does not disappoint.

www.ingramcontent.com/pod-product-compliance
Lightning Source LLC
Chambersburg PA
CBHW021451080526
44588CB00009B/792